WIGAN & LEIGH
COLLEGE

Children's
FIRST
Book of
PEOPLE AND PLACES

Children's
FIRST
Book of
PEOPLE AND PLACES

p

Author and Editor
Neil Morris

Projects created by
Ting Morris

Art Direction
Full Steam Ahead Ltd

Designer
Branka Surla

Project Management
Rosie Alexander

Artwork commissioned by
Branka Surla

Picture Research
Rosie Alexander, Kate Miles, Elaine Willis, Yannick Yago

Editorial Assistant
Lynne French

Additional editorial help from
Suzanne Airey, Hilary Bird, Paul Kilgour, Jenny Sharman

Editorial Director
Jim Miles

The publishers would like to thank the following people for their help:
Jenni Cozens, Pat Crisp, Ian Paulyn

This is a Parragon Book
This edition published in 2000

Parragon
Queen Street House
4 Queen Street
Bath BA1 1HE, UK

Produced by Miles Kelly Publishing Ltd
Unit 11, Bardfield Centre, Great Bardfield, Essex CM7 4SL

ISBN 0-75254-298-2

Printed in Dubai, U.A.E.

Contents

How to use this book

In this book, every page is filled with information on the sort of topics that you will enjoy reading about.

Information is given in photographs and illustrations, as well as in words. All the pictures are explained by captions, to tell you what you are looking at and to give even more detailed facts.

The **cartoons** throughout the book are not always meant to be taken too seriously! They are supposed to be fun, but the text that goes with them gives real information.

Captions beginning with a symbol give extra pieces of information that you will find interesting.

Project boxes describe craft activities related to the topic. These are things to make or simple experiments to do. The photograph helps to show you what to do, and is there to inspire you to have a go! But remember, some of the activities can be quite messy, so put old newspaper down first. Always use round-ended scissors, and ask an adult for help if you are unsure of something or need sharp tools or materials.

Illustrations are clear and simple, and sometimes they are cut away so that you can see inside things. The triangle at the beginning of the caption text points to the illustration concerned.

The main text on each double-page spread gives a short introduction to that particular topic. Every time you turn the page, you will find a new topic.

Beautiful photographs have been specially chosen to bring each subject to life. The caption triangle points to the right photograph.

A New Words box appears on every double-page spread. This list explains some difficult words and technical terms.

There are maps in many sections, which show the particular region discussed in that topic.

South American People

The first Europeans arrived in South America in the 16th century. They then conquered and destroyed the powerful native American cultures they found there. The cultures included that of the mighty Inca empire.

Today, most South Americans are descended from Europeans and Indians, or native Americans, and many are a mixture of the two. Spanish is the continent's main language, but in the largest country, Brazil, people speak Portuguese. Native Americans also speak hundreds of Indian languages.

NEW WORDS
carnival A large festival with processions and fancy dress.
gaucho A cowboy and cattleman of Argentina.
native American The original people of North and South America, sometimes called Indians.
pampas Flat grassy lands of Argentina.

MAKE A SHAKER
Use an empty washing-up liquid bottle or similar. Put in some dried beans and push a stick into the neck of the bottle. Tape the stick so that it fits tightly. Paint the shaker with powder or poster paints mixed with a teaspoon of washing-up liquid. Stick on some tissue-paper decorations with PVA glue. Then shake to a South American beat.

▽ **The Aymara people** traditionally live by farming and fishing from reed boats in Lake Titicaca. The lake lies high in the Andes, between Peru and Bolivia.

△ **Brazil** is famous for its friendly, crowded carnivals. They draw thousands of tourists every year. Many of the locals dress up in colourful costumes.

◇ **Soccer** is the most popular sport in South America. Brazil has won the World Cup four times, and Uruguay and Argentina twice each.

▽ **Gauchos** are Argentinian cowboys, famous for their horsemanship. They herd cattle on grassy plains called pampas.

◇ **Many people** of the Amazon rainforest are losing their homeland as trees are cut down for timber and grazing land.

Big or Little Rain! So much rain falls in the rainforest around the Amazon that Brazilians divide the seasons into times of "big rain" and "little rain". All this rain means that more than one fifth of all the water in the world's rivers flows down the River Amazon.

▽ **The mountain people** of the Andes spin the wool they get from their llamas and sheep into yarn. Then they weave the yarn into brightly coloured shawls, skirts and blankets using traditional designs.

People and Places

The people of the world live on six different continents. Each of these continents has its own special landscapes and famous places, all of which have developed in their own unique way thoughout history. Humans live in rainforests and deserts, near oceans and rivers, in small villages as well as gigantic, crowded cities.

All the world's people belong to the same human race, despite being split up into hundreds of nations and other groups. Many of these groups have their own language, religion, festivals and customs, all based on their own special history. We can all learn by studying how other people live, all over the world.

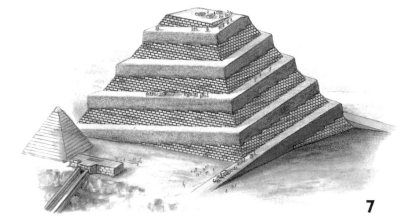

North America

◁ **The Grand Canyon,** in Arizona, USA, is the largest gorge in the world. It is about 350 km long and 2 km deep.

NEW WORDS
arc A curved shape.
borough A district or part of a city.
gorge A deep valley with steep sides.
icecap A permanent covering of ice in a region.
prairie A large area of flat grassland.

The continent of North America stretches all the way from the frozen Arctic Ocean in the north to the warm waters of the Caribbean Sea in the south. It includes two of the biggest countries in the world, Canada and the United States of America.

The land varies from the freezing icecaps of Greenland to the huge cold forests of Canada, from the American prairies and the deserts of northern Mexico, to the tropical rainforests of Central America. The Rocky Mountains run almost all the way down the western side of the continent, whilst New York City – the largest city in the United States – is on the eastern side.

▽ **The skyscraper city** of New York. The crowded island of Manhattan, one of the city's five boroughs, is surrounded by three rivers. Bridges and tunnels link it with the rest of the city.

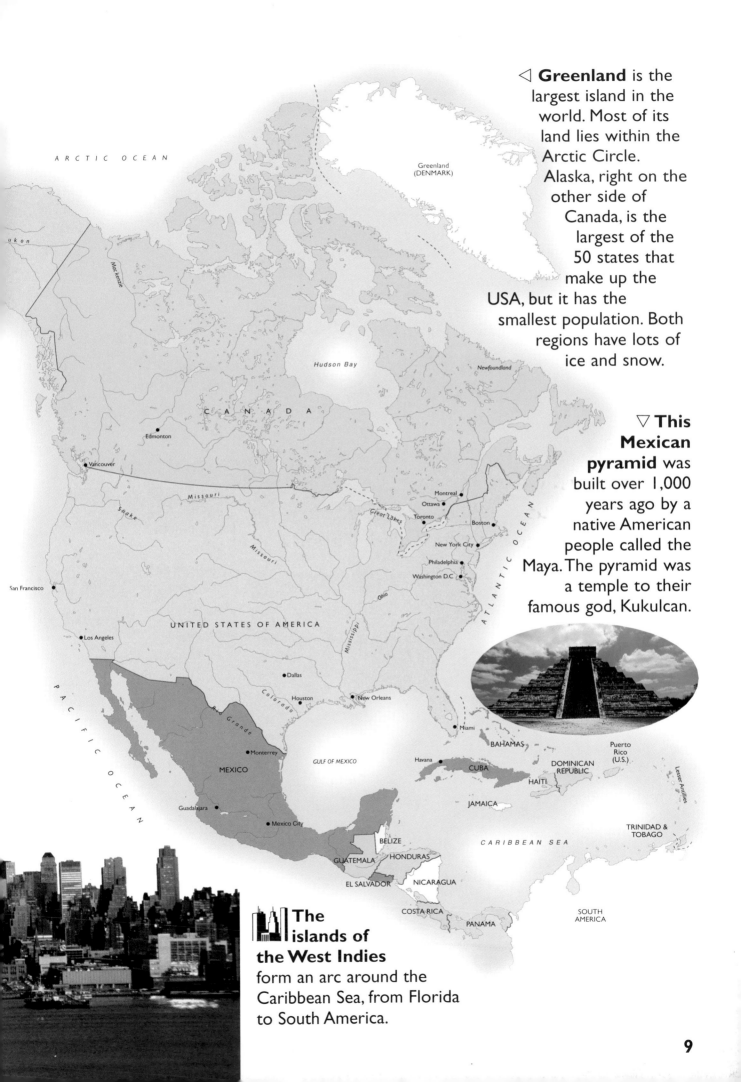

◁ **Greenland** is the largest island in the world. Most of its land lies within the Arctic Circle. Alaska, right on the other side of Canada, is the largest of the 50 states that make up the USA, but it has the smallest population. Both regions have lots of ice and snow.

▽ **This Mexican pyramid** was built over 1,000 years ago by a native American people called the Maya. The pyramid was a temple to their famous god, Kukulcan.

The islands of the West Indies form an arc around the Caribbean Sea, from Florida to South America.

ARCTIC OCEAN

Greenland
(DENMARK)

uk o n

Mac Kenzie

Hudson Bay

Newfoundland

C A N A D A

Edmonton

Vancouver

Missouri

Snake

Montreal

Ottawa

Toronto

Great Lakes

Boston

New York City

Philadelphia

Washington D.C

Missouri

Mississippi

Ohio

ATLANTIC OCEAN

San Francisco

UNITED STATES OF AMERICA

Los Angeles

Dallas

Colorado

Houston

New Orleans

Miami

PACIFIC OCEAN

Rio Grande

Monterrey

MEXICO

GULF OF MEXICO

Havana

BAHAMAS

CUBA

DOMINICAN
REPUBLIC

Puerto
Rico
(U.S.)

HAITI

Lesser Antilles

JAMAICA

Guadalajara

Mexico City

TRINIDAD &
TOBAGO

BELIZE

CARIBBEAN SEA

GUATEMALA

HONDURAS

EL SALVADOR

NICARAGUA

COSTA RICA

PANAMA

SOUTH
AMERICA

North American People

△ **The Inuit** live in the very north of the continent, in northern Canada and Greenland. In their own language, Inuit just means people.

Many thousands of years ago, hunters from north-east Asia crossed a land bridge to the region that is now called Alaska. These native Americans gradually spread southwards, across the whole of the continent.

About 1,000 years ago, Viking explorers sailed to North America from Europe. But it was less than 500 years ago that Europeans first made permanent settlements there.

Today, the USA forms a single nation with its own way of life, but it is made up of people who came to live there from all over the world. This is what we call a "multi-cultural society".

◁ **Riding a bucking bronco** is one of the tests an American cowboy has to go through at a rodeo. The cowboy tries to stay on the horse for as long as he can.

Years ago, cowboys drove huge herds of cattle to railway towns. This was a hard life and not nearly as exciting as it looks in cowboy films!

On the fourth Thursday in November, Americans celebrate Thanksgiving. Early settlers "gave thanks" for surviving in the New World.

When and where was the US railroad completed?
On May 10, 1869, a Union Pacific construction locomotive met one from the Central Pacific line, at a place called Promontory, in Utah. This completed a track that ran right across the United States.

▽ **Mexicans** celebrate many public holidays with a "fiesta". Then the streets are crowded with people.

△ **Native Americans** who lived along the north-west Pacific coast of Canada and the USA carved beautiful totem poles outside their homes.

▷ **American football** is a hard, physical sport. Players have to be protected by pads and helmets. Every year teams play for the Super Bowl.

FEATHER HEADDRESS
Cut a strip of corrugated paper and fit it around your head. Then stick the ends together with parcel tape. Tear coloured tissue into small pieces, crumple the pieces up and glue them to the outside. Cut feather shapes from tissue and glue each one onto a plastic straw. Slot the ends into the corrugated holes to complete your headdress.

South America

The continent of South America is divided into 13 countries. By far the largest of these countries is Brazil, which covers nearly half the continent's total area.

The Andes Mountains stretch down almost the whole of South America. They form the longest mountain range in the world. The great Amazon River begins high in the Andes of Peru. It flows across the plains of Brazil, through the world's biggest rainforest, to the Atlantic Ocean.

▷ **The Andes** mountain range is 7,200 km long. The highest point, called Aconcagua, is in Argentina.

▷ **The ruins** of the Inca town of Machu Picchu are perched high above a river valley in the Andes of Peru. A royal palace and a temple are among the ruins.

◁ **A huge statue of Christ** looks down on the city and crowded beaches of Rio de Janeiro, in Brazil. The statue is 40 m high.

▽ **Llamas** are members of the camel family. They have been herded in Peru for thousands of years, for their wool and to carry things.

12

The Angel Falls, in Venezuela, is. the world's highest waterfall, falling to a depth of 979 m.

▽ **In the thick Amazonian rainforest,** parrots and toucans feed in the treetops, while monkeys swing through the branches of this leafy canopy.

Brazil is the world's biggest producer of oranges, bananas, coffee and sugarcane.

◁ **The southern tip of the continent** is called Cape Horn. It was named in 1616 by a Dutch explorer, after his home town of Hoorn in Holland. The Cape is usually very stormy.

The Atacama Desert stretches for almost 1,000 km along the Pacific coast of Chile. This is thought to be the driest place on Earth, because there is hardly ever any recorded rainfall at all.

NEW WORDS

plain A landscape with few trees.

range A group of mountains side by side.

13

South American People

The first Europeans arrived in South America in the 16th century. They then conquered and destroyed the powerful native American cultures they found there. The cultures included that of the mighty Inca empire.

Today, most South Americans are descended from Europeans and Indians, or native Americans, and many are a mixture of the two. Spanish is the continent's main language, but in the largest country, Brazil, people speak Portuguese. Native Americans also speak hundreds of Indian languages.

NEW WORDS

🪐 **carnival** A large festival with processions and fancy dress.

🪐 **gaucho** A cowboy and cattleman of Argentina.

🪐 **native Americans** The original people of North and South America, sometimes called Indians.

🪐 **pampas** Flat grassy lands of Argentina.

▽ **The Aymara people** traditionally live by farming and fishing from reed boats in Lake Titicaca. The lake lies high in the Andes, between Peru and Bolivia.

△ **Brazil** is famous for its friendly, crowded carnivals. They draw thousands of tourists every year. Many of the locals dress up in colourful costumes.

MAKE A SHAKER
Use an empty washing-up liquid bottle or similar. Put in some dried beans and push a stick into the neck of the bottle. Tape the stick so that it fits tightly. Paint the shaker with powder or poster paints mixed with a teaspoon of washing-up liquid. Stick on some tissue-paper decorations with PVA glue. Then shake to a South American beat.

Many people of the Amazon rainforest are losing their homeland as trees are cut down for timber and grazing land.

Big or Little Rain?
So much rain falls in the rainforest around the Amazon that Brazilians divide the seasons into times of "big rains" and "little rains". All this rain means that more than one fifth of all the water in the world's rivers flows down the River Amazon.

Soccer is the most popular sport in South America. Brazil has won the World Cup four times, and Uruguay and Argentina twice each.

▽ **Gauchos** are Argentinian cowboys, famous for their horsemanship. They herd cattle on grassy plains called pampas.

◁ **The mountain people** of the Andes spin the wool they get from their llamas and sheep into yarn. Then they weave the yarn into brightly coloured shawls, skirts and blankets using traditional designs.

15

Europe

The northern parts of Europe are mainly cold regions. They include Scandinavia, which is made up of Norway, Sweden, Finland, Denmark and Iceland.

The central parts of the continent are mild, while the southern regions surrounding the Mediterranean Sea are mainly warm and dry. Europe has a rugged coastline, dotted with islands.

△ **In the Middle Ages,** important Europeans defended themselves in castles. Europe has many different types of castles.

Is the Black Sea black?
The waters of the Black Sea are not black, and it is a favourite holiday region. It may have got its name because heavy fog and sudden storms sometimes make it look dark. The ancient Romans called it the "Friendly Sea"!

▷ **There are many** active geysers, or hot springs, in Iceland. They regularly throw boiling hot water and steam high up into the air.

Icelanders use hot water from beneath the Earth's surface to run power stations and heat their homes.

REP.

◁ **The road across Tower Bridge,** in London, can open in the middle and swing up in the air. It does this so that tall ships can pass through and carry on up the River Thames. The rivers of Europe are important waterways.

PORTUGAL
Lisbon

◁ **A popular tourist beach** on one of the many small islands off the mainland of Greece. In the summer it is warm and sunny all the way around the coast of the Mediterranean Sea.

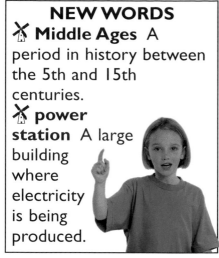

NEW WORDS
✠ **Middle Ages** A period in history between the 5th and 15th centuries.
✠ **power station** A large building where electricity is being produced.

▷ **The Ural Mountains,** running across Russia, form an imaginary line separating the continents of Europe and Asia. Europe is well-known for its trade and industry.

NORWEGIAN SEA

ATLANTIC OCEAN

ICELAND

SWEDEN
NORWAY
FINLAND
Helsinki
Oslo
Stockholm
St. Petersburg
Archangel
RUSSIA
Nizhniy Novgorod
Moscow

NORTH SEA

DENMARK
Copenhagen
ESTONIA
LATVIA
LITHUANIA
BALTIC SEA

IRELAND
Dublin

UNITED KINGDOM
London
NETHERLANDS
BELGIUM
Berlin
Warsaw
Minsk
BELARUS
GERMANY
POLAND
Kiev
UKRAINE
Dnieper
Don
KAZAKHSTAN
Volga

Paris
Seine
Loire
LUXEMBOURG
CZECH REPUBLIC
SLOVAKIA
Danube
Vienna
MOLDOVA
FRANCE
Lyon
AUSTRIA
Budapest
HUNGARY
ROMANIA
SWITZERLAND
Rhône
Milan
Po
SLOVENIA
CROATIA
Bucharest
BLACK SEA

Bay of Biscay

ANDORRA
Barcelona
Corsica
ITALY
BOSNIA HERZEGOVINA
YUGOSLAVIA
BULGARIA
Sofia
Rome
MACEDONIA
Istanbul
Sardinia
Naples
ALBANIA
Ankara
TURKEY
Balearic Islands (Spain)
GREECE

MEDITERRANEAN
Sicily
Athens
ASIA

NORTH AFRICA

SPAIN

▽ **Marching military bands** are a traditional feature of British ceremonies and special events. These soldiers are wearing fur helmets known as bearskins.

▷ **A gondolier,** or oarsman, rows his gondola along one of the many canals of Venice, in northern Italy. The water almost completely surrounds this beautiful city.

NEW WORDS

bearskin A tall fur hat worn by some soldiers as part of their uniform.

culture Customs and traditions.

gondola A boat with high pointed ends that is rowed in Venice.

Latin The language of the ancient Romans, which some people still learn at school.

Pope The leader of the Roman Catholic Church.

▽ **The grape harvest** is very important to many farmers and winemakers in France, Italy, Spain and other southern European countries. In the past, people trod on the grapes to press out the juice, but today the pressing is usually done by a special machine.

European People

Europe is full of many small countries and different peoples, most of whom have their own language and culture.

The north is home to Finns and Lapps, and to those who speak Germanic languages, such as the English, Dutch and Germans. In the south, the French, Spanish and Italian languages all came from Latin, the language of the ancient Romans.

◁ **Flamenco** is a Spanish way of dancing and singing to guitar music. Dancers snap their fingers, clap their hands and shout to the rhythmic music.

△ **This square** is in Prague, the capital and largest city of the Czech Republic. The city's historic buildings attract many visitors all year round.

 **The world's smallest country** is called Vatican City. It is the home of the Pope and lies in Rome, the capital of Italy.

FAN YOURSELF

To make a Spanish fan, first paint or draw a bright pattern on a long sheet of paper. You could decorate it with glitter glue to add extra sparkle. When it's dry, fold the paper into a concertina, with the folds all the same size. Staple the folds at one end and then attach a lolly stick as a handle for your fancy fan.

19

Asia

Asia is by far the largest continent in the world, bigger than the whole of North and South America added together.

The Asian landscape varies from the huge, cold forest that stretches across northern Russia to the warm, wet rainforests of the islands of Southeast Asia. The world's highest mountains are also to be found in Asia.

△ **Rice** is an important food throughout Asia. It is grown in flooded paddy fields, like this one in Thailand. Sometimes fields are drained to help with harvesting.

▽ **The Himalayas,** a mountain range to the north of India, contain many of the highest mountains in the world. The highest of all is Mount Everest, which rises to a height of about 8,848 m.

◁ **Hong Kong** is an important port and city on the Chinese coast. This former British colony was returned to China in 1997.

▷ **The Great Wall of China** was built to help keep out invaders from the north. It was begun in about 200 BC.

Russia is the largest country in the world. The Trans-Siberian Railway runs all the way from the Russian capital, Moscow, to Beijing, the capital of China.

Where is the land of the rising sun?
The Japanese name for Japan, Nippon, means "source of the sun". A legend tells how an ancient god dipped his spear into the ocean and formed the islands of Japan from the sunlit droplets of water.

ARCTIC OCEAN

Bering Sea

PACIFIC OCEAN

EUROPE

Tunguska

R U S S I A

Yekaterinburg

Black Sea

Ankara
TURKEY

GEORGIA

CYPRUS

ARMENIA
AZERBAIJAN

LEBANON
ISRAEL   SYRIA
JORDAN

Baghdad
IRAQ

SAUDI
ARABIA

KUWAIT

BAHRAIN
QATAR
Riyadh
UNITED
ARAB
EMIRATES

Mecca

Sana

YEMEN   OMAN

Muscat

AFRICA

Nile

Red Sea

Euphrates
Tigris

I R A N

Tehran

TURKMENISTAN

Amu Dar'ya

Caspian Sea

Aqmola

KAZAKHSTAN

Syr Dar'ya

Irtysh

UZBEKISTAN

Almaty

KYRGYZSTAN

TAJIKISTAN

AFGHANISTAN

Islamabad

PAKISTAN

Indus

New Delhi

NEPAL

BHUTAN

Ganges

BANGLADESH

Calcutta

I N D I A

Bombay

Godavari

Madras

Colombo

SRI
LANKA

Arabian Sea

Novosibirsk

Ob'

Yenisey

Lena

Indigirka

Lake Baikal

Ulan Bator

M O N G O L I A

Amur

Shenyang   NORTH
KOREA

Beijing

SOUTH
KOREA

Tokyo

J A P A N

C H I N A

Huang

Chang

TAIWAN

Hong Kong

Macao (Port.)

BURMA   LAOS

Yangon

THAILAND

CAMBODIA VIETNAM

Manila

PHILIPPINES

BRUNEI

Irian Jaya

MALAYSIA

SINGAPORE

Borneo

Celebes

I N D O N E S I A

Sumatra

Jankara   Java

INDIAN OCEAN

▷ **Japan** has more than 3,900 islands. Most of the islands of Southeast Asia are part of either the Philippines or of Indonesia.

21

AUSTRALIA

Asian People

Over half the world's people live in Asia, which includes the country with more people than any other – China. The world's first civilizations grew up in southwest Asia. In a fertile area between two great rivers, people grew crops and built big cities.

△ **The Mongols** of northern China and Mongolia are expert horse riders. They follow their herds of goats and cattle across the grasslands, living in felt tents called yurts.

NEW WORDS
fertile With rich soil, producing good crops.
nomads People who wander from place to place to find food and grazing land.
yurt A felt tent built and carried around by the Mongol people.

JAPANESE BEAUTY

You can easily make a simple Japanese flower arrangement in a bowl. Cover the bottom of the clear bowl with soil, then add gravel, shells and pebbles. Push a small twig through the gravel into the soil. Half-fill the bowl with water. Then decorate the surface with leaves and flowers, to make simple Japanese beauty.

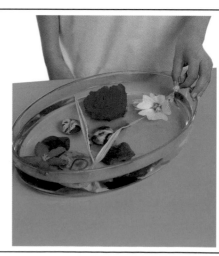

▷ **Very few people** live in the dry, hot Arabian Desert, but some Bedouin nomads wander around its edges. They herd camels and cattle, and live in dark tents.

Mount Everest lies between Nepal and Tibet. It was first climbed in 1953, by a Nepalese Sherpa called Tenzing Norgay and the New Zealander, Sir Edmund Hillary.

▽ **Fishermen** in Sri Lanka sit on pole perches in the shallow sea to fish.

△ **In China,** cycling is a very popular way to get around the big cities quickly and easily. There are many large bicycle parks, with special attendants to look after them.

The Sultan of Brunei is said be the richest person in the world. He lives in a palace with 1,788 rooms. Brunei is a small country on the island of Borneo.

In Indonesia, on the island of Borneo, many families of the Dayak people live together in wooden longhouses.

▷ **Sumo** is the national wrestling sport of Japan. Sumo wrestlers are very big and strong, and they try to throw down their opponent or force him out of the ring to win.

23

Africa

Africa is the world's second largest continent. It is made up of 53 independent countries, some large and others small. The largest African country, Sudan, is over 200 times bigger then the smallest, Gambia.

The biggest desert in the world, the Sahara, covers more than a quarter of the continent. It stretches over 5,000 km from the Atlantic Ocean to the Red Sea. Further south, the land is much more fertile and there are rainforests and grasslands.

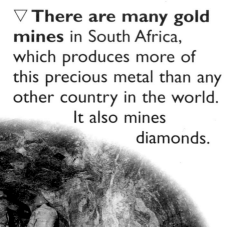

▽ **There are many gold mines** in South Africa, which produces more of this precious metal than any other country in the world. It also mines diamonds.

▽ **Beautiful Egyptian boats** called feluccas sail on the River Nile, the longest river in the world. The Nile brings water and life to the desert countries that it flows through.

In 1869 the Suez Canal was opened, joining the Red Sea to the Mediterranean Sea. This meant that ships could sail from Europe to the Indian Ocean without having to go right round Africa and the Cape of Good Hope. The canal is 169 km long and thousands of ships pass through it every year.

NEW WORD
felucca An Egyptian boat with one triangular sail.

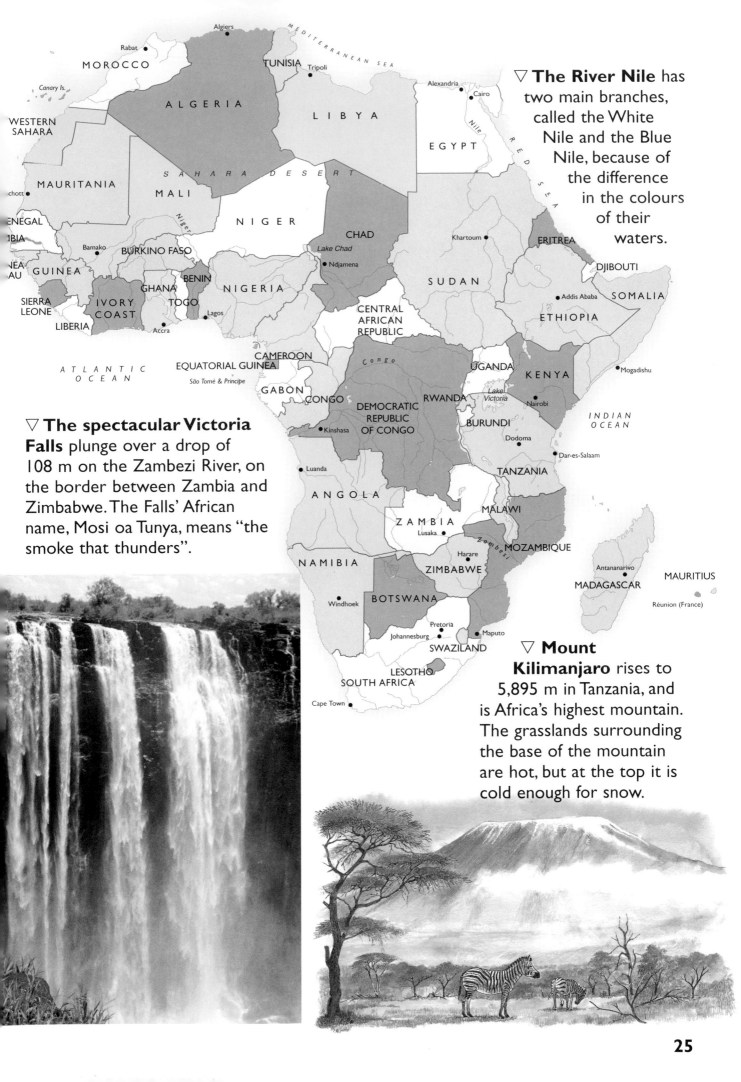

MEDITERRANEAN SEA

MOROCCO
Rabat
Algiers
TUNISIA
Tripoli
ALGERIA
LIBYA
Alexandria
Cairo
EGYPT
Canary Is.
WESTERN SAHARA
SAHARA DESERT
RED SEA
Nile
MAURITANIA
MALI
NIGER
CHAD
Khartoum
ERITREA
chott
Lake Chad
DJIBOUTI
Bamako
BURKINO FASO
Ndjamena
ENEGAL
Niger
BENIN
SUDAN
Addis Ababa
SOMALIA
IBIA
GHANA
NIGERIA
CENTRAL AFRICAN REPUBLIC
ETHIOPIA
NEA
AU
GUINEA
IVORY COAST
TOGO
Lagos
SIERRA LEONE
LIBERIA
Accra
CAMEROON
EQUATORIAL GUINEA
ATLANTIC OCEAN
São Tomé & Principe
Congo
UGANDA
KENYA
Mogadishu
GABON
CONGO
DEMOCRATIC REPUBLIC OF CONGO
RWANDA
Lake Victoria
Nairobi
INDIAN OCEAN
Kinshasa
BURUNDI
Dodoma
Luanda
Dar-es-Salaam
TANZANIA
ANGOLA
MALAWI
ZAMBIA
Lusaka
Zambezi
MOZAMBIQUE
Antananarivo
MAURITIUS
NAMIBIA
Harare
ZIMBABWE
MADAGASCAR
Réunion (France)
Windhoek
BOTSWANA
Pretoria
Maputo
Johannesburg
SWAZILAND
LESOTHO
SOUTH AFRICA
Cape Town

▽ **The River Nile** has two main branches, called the White Nile and the Blue Nile, because of the difference in the colours of their waters.

▽ **The spectacular Victoria Falls** plunge over a drop of 108 m on the Zambezi River, on the border between Zambia and Zimbabwe. The Falls' African name, Mosi oa Tunya, means "the smoke that thunders".

▽ **Mount Kilimanjaro** rises to 5,895 m in Tanzania, and is Africa's highest mountain. The grasslands surrounding the base of the mountain are hot, but at the top it is cold enough for snow.

25

African People

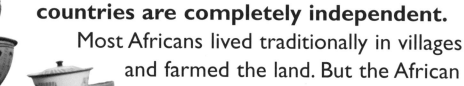

▽ **These women** belong to a people called the Fulani, who live in West Africa. Many Fulani are still cattle-herders, as they always have been, while others have moved to the cities for work.

Scientists believe that the earliest humans lived in Africa, millions of years ago. In more recent times, many African tribes and their lands were controlled by Europeans. Today, most African countries are completely independent.

△ **Many Africans** still dress in a traditional way, according to the custom of their tribe.

Most Africans lived traditionally in villages and farmed the land. But the African population is growing very quickly, and many large cities have sprung up and continue to grow. Here there are modern offices and factories.

NEW WORDS

independent Governing itself and not controlled by other people.

pygmies Members of various groups of small people.

tribe A group of people from the same race and with the same customs.

▷ **The streets** of many north African towns and cities are very crowded, and there are bustling markets. Marrakech, a large city in Morocco, is well known for its leather goods and textiles. These, and the warm climate, make it popular with tourists.

▽ **Johannesburg** is the largest city in South Africa and about four million people live there. It has many modern skyscrapers and shopping centres.

△ **Camels** are sometimes called the "ships of the desert", because they can go for a long time without water. Their humps are large stores of fat. Camels are a useful means of transport for people, and can travel as far as 160 km in a day.

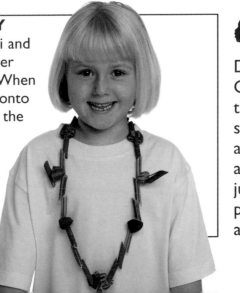

AFRICAN JEWELLERY
Use felt pens to colour macaroni and pasta wheels in stripes. Paint other pasta shapes with poster paints. When the shapes are dry, thread them onto about a metre of ribbon, varying the order of the shapes to make it look more interesting. Then try the necklace on – it should be easy to slip on and off. Finally, tie the ends of the ribbon with a double knot.

The Mbuti pygmies who live in the Democratic Republic of the Congo (formerly Zaire) are thought to be the world's shortest people. The average man is 1.45 m tall, and some Mbuti women are just 1.24 m. The Masai people of East Africa are among the tallest Africans.

Which lake has no water?

Lake Eyre, Australia's largest lake, is normally a huge area of mud covered with a crust of salt. This is because it is so hot and dry in the desert lands of South Australia. When there is very heavy rainfall, the lake does fill with water, but this is quite rare.

The Pacific Islands are in three main groups — Micronesia, which means "small islands", Melanesia ("black islands") and, finally, Polynesia meaning "many islands".

▽ **Ayers Rock** rises 348 m above the surrounding dry plain in the Northern Territory. This giant rock is sacred to the Aborigines, who call it Uluru, which means "Earth mother".

HAWAIIAN ISLANDS (U.S.)

Northern Marianas (U.S.)

MARSHALL ISLANDS

PHILIPPINES

PACIFIC OCEAN

FEDERATION STATES OF INDONESIA

Celebes Sea

PAPUA NEW GUINEA

KIRIBATI

INDONESIA

SOLOMON ISLANDS

TUVALU

Tokelau (New Zealand)

Cook Islands (New Zealand)

Darwin

Coral Sea

VANUATU

FIJI

SAMOA

American Samoa

AUSTRALIA

Alice Springs

TONGA

NEW CALEDONIA

Perth

Brisbane

Darling

Adelaide

Sydney

Canberra

Aukland

Melbourne

Tasman Sea

Wellington

Tasmania

NEW ZEALAND

Australasia

Aborigines The original people of Australia.

coral reef A large ridge in warm, shallow waters made up of a colony of tiny animals called corals.

outback The bush country of Australia, where desert land is partly covered by bushes and some trees.

The continent of Australasia is made up of Australia, New Zealand, Papua New Guinea and thousands of small islands in the South Pacific Ocean. This region is sometimes called Oceania.

Australia is a warm, dry country and much of its land is desert and dry bush country, called outback. New Zealand has a milder climate. Both countries are home to many plants and animals seen nowhere else on Earth. The Pacific Islands cover a vast area, but most of them are very small.

△ **The roof** of the Sydney Opera House looks like giant sails. Sydney is the oldest and biggest city in Australia.

▷ **The Great Barrier Reef** lies off the coast of Australia. It is made up of thousands of coral reefs. The warm, shallow water is home to colourful fish.

Papua New Guinea covers the eastern half of New Guinea. The western half, called Irian Jaya, belongs to Indonesia.

Corals look like plants, but they are really made up of tiny, colourful animals. They are related to jellyfish.

29

Australasian People

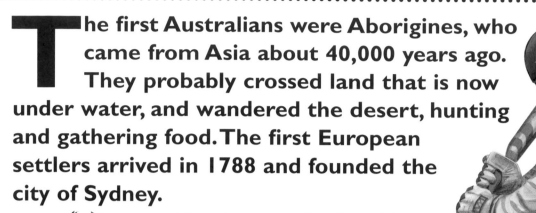

The first Australians were Aborigines, who came from Asia about 40,000 years ago. They probably crossed land that is now under water, and wandered the desert, hunting and gathering food. The first European settlers arrived in 1788 and founded the city of Sydney.

Maoris were the first New Zealanders. According to a Maori legend, they sailed there from Polynesian islands in just seven canoes.

◁ **Aborigines** play a long, thick wooden pipe called a didgeridoo. This makes a deep note, and sometimes the player rests the pipe on a hole in the ground to make it sound louder. A boomerang, or throwing stick, is another traditional item.

△ **Cricket** is a very popular sport in Australia and New Zealand. Many celebrated batsmen and bowlers have come from those two countries.

Australia is the sixth biggest country in the world, but only 18 million people live there. Much of the land is hot, dry desert but most people live along the coasts.

PLAY A PIPE

Poke holes into one side of a cardboard tube. Then paint the tube. When it's dry, cover one end with greaseproof paper, holding it in place with a rubber band. To play your pipe, hum into the open end as you move your fingers over the holes. A longer pipe makes a deeper note.

▽ **Australian Aborigines** tell stories in their rock paintings. Many have been found that are thousands of years old.

▽ **Wood carving** is a traditional craft of the Maoris of New Zealand. The carvings decorate Maori meeting houses. Today, much of the work is done to sell to tourists.

△ **Many people** of the New Guinea highlands traditionally paint their bodies for special ceremonies. They make colours from earth and wear mud masks and headdresses.

What day is it?
The international date line is an imaginary line that runs between the Pacific islands. On the western side of the line, it is exactly a day later than on the eastern side. So when it is midday Friday in Fiji, it is midday Thursday in Western Samoa.

NEW WORDS
⌐ **didgeridoo** A long, hollow, wooden pipe played by Aborigines.
⌐ **Maoris** The original people of New Zealand.
⌐ **pidgin English** A simple form of the English language.

◁ **Modern Australians** love the outdoor life. Surfing is popular off many beaches, along with swimming and sailing.

⌐ **The various peoples** of Papua New Guinea speak more than 700 different languages. Pidgin English and Motu are the most common languages.

MAKE A MUMMY

Take a doll and an old sheet. Tear the sheet into strips and wrap the doll from head to toe in these bandages. Make a coffin from a shoebox. The Egyptians put green stone scarab beetles along with their mummies, and you could paint one on the end of the coffin. When you want your doll back, just take the bandages off your Egyptian mummy!

⚠ When a body was mummified, the dead person's internal organs (liver, lungs, stomach and intestines) were removed and stored in special jars.

⚠ Cats were sacred to the ancient Egyptians and were also mummified when they died.

▷ **It probably took 100,000 men** over 20 years to build the Great Pyramid. They used over two million heavy blocks of stone. The pharaoh's burial chamber was deep inside the pyramid.

▽ **The wall-paintings** found in ancient tombs have told us a lot about the way ancient Egyptians lived.

▷ **Pharaohs** were sometimes buried inside huge stone pyramids. The Great Pyramid is still standing at Giza, near Cairo, the modern capital of Egypt.

Ancient Egypt

Thousands of years ago, people hunted around the River Nile. Then they settled there and began to farm the land.

Ancient Egypt was ruled by kings, called pharaohs. The Egyptians believed the spirit of their hawk god, Horus, entered a new pharaoh and made him a god too. They also believed in life after death, and pharaohs were buried with things they wanted to take on to the next world.

△ **Egyptian noblemen** hunted in the marshes around the Nile. They used throwing sticks to bring down birds.

NEW WORDS

mummy A dead body specially treated so that it does not decay.

pharaoh A king of ancient Egypt.

tomb A place where someone is buried.

▷ **King Tutankhamun** died at only 18 years old. He was buried in a tomb in the Valley of the Kings, near the ancient city of Thebes. This gold mask was found among the treasure in Tutankhamun's tomb.

◁ **The stone monument** of the Great Sphinx has a man's head and a lion's body. It stands 20 m high, near the pyramids at Giza. The Sphinx was carved 4,500 years ago.

Ancient Greece

Hermes   Aphrodite   Zeus   Hera   Demeter   Hades

◁ **Zeus** was king of the Greek gods, and Hera was his wife. Hermes was the gods' messenger, Aphrodite was the goddess of love, Demeter goddess of grain, and Hades god of the dead.

About 2,800 years ago, a new civilization began in Greece. The ancient Greeks produced many fine buildings and cities. They wrote plays, studied music and began a system of government which allowed people a say in how their state was run.

Athens became the biggest and richest city state in ancient Greece, with a very well-trained army and a powerful navy. Sparta controlled the southern part of Greece. All true Spartans had to be warriors, and boys were trained to fight from the age of seven.

NEW WORDS

city state A state made up of a city and the surrounding areas.
column A pillar used to hold up a building.
government The ruling and running of a state or country.
state An organized community, such as a country.
trireme A warship with three banks of oars on each side.

◁ **The Parthenon** was the main temple of the goddess Athene. Today, its ruins stand on a rocky hill in Athens called the Acropolis.

▷ **The Greeks** were the first to build permanent stone theatres. In ancient times the actors were all men, and they wore masks to show the sort of character they were playing.

Corinthian

Ionic

Doric

◁ **The ancient Greeks** developed special ways to decorate the tops of the columns, or pillars, that they used to support their beautiful buildings. Doric was the earliest order, or type. Then came Ionic, and finally Corinthian.

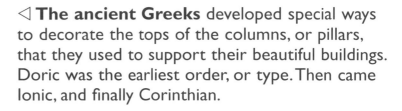

When and where were the first Olympic Games?
The first Olympic Games were held in 776 BC in Olympia, a place dedicated to the god Zeus. The first athletes carried shields and wore helmets, but no clothes!

DRAMATIC MASKS
Put a dinner plate on card and draw around it. Then cut out the circle. Hold the card in front of your face and ask a friend to mark carefully the position of your eyes. Put the card down and cut out two eye holes to see through. Paint a happy or a sad face, and tape on a lolly-stick handle. Finally, stick on card ears and ribbon hair.

Rich Greek boys had their own slave. It was his job to look after the boy, take him to school and help with his homework.

▷ **The most famous** types of Greek warship were biremes and triremes. A bireme had two banks of rowers on each side, and a trireme had three banks. Soldiers fought on the flat deck of the ships, which could go very fast and be used to ram others.

Ancient Rome

The great city of Rome began as a small village on one of seven hills, over 2,700 years ago. As the city grew in size and power, the Romans conquered other peoples in Italy.

Then the Roman armies created an empire that stretched around the Mediterranean Sea and reached as far as France and England. Roman soldiers built thousands of kilometres of good, straight roads throughout their empire. Some Roman roads still exist to this day.

▷ **The Roman Empire** began under Augustus, who became the first emperor in 27 BC. This great leader set the style for later emperors.

△ **In AD 79,** Mount Vesuvius suddenly erupted and covered the nearby Italian town of Pompeii with volcanic ash. The town was buried and thousands of people were killed.

According to legend, Rome was founded by two twins, Romulus and Remus. Abandoned as babies, the brothers were fed milk by a female wolf and later found by a shepherd.

Roman cities always had fresh water. It was brought from the hills to street fountains and houses along aqueducts.

What was the Roman circus?
In ancient Rome, the circus was an oval-shaped arena where chariot races were held. These were very popular sporting events, and up to 250,000 people could pack into the biggest circus in Rome.

▷ **Julius Caesar** was a great Roman general in the last years before the first emperor. He was stabbed to death in 44 BC.

▽ **The Forum** in ancient Rome was an open public square. Citizens went there to discuss any important questions of the day together.

▽ **The Colosseum** was the largest amphitheatre of ancient Rome. It could hold about 50,000 spectators.

▷ **Centurions** were officers in the Roman army. Each one commanded about a hundred soldiers, who made up a century. The army was very well trained and extremely powerful.

The Middle Ages

T he Middle Ages is the name that is usually given to roughly a thousand years of history, starting in about AD 500. This medieval period covers the history between ancient and modern times in Europe.

During the Middle Ages, European countries were ruled by a king or an emperor, who generally owned all the land. The land was divided among the ruler's most important men, who were called nobles. The nobles were supported by knights, who were trained in battle. Peasants lived and worked on the nobles' and knights' land, growing food for both themselves and for their lord.

△ **Printing** had not yet been invented. Books were copied by hand by monks. They were often beautifully decorated in bright colours.

▽ **Kings and nobles** built castles to protect themselves against enemies. Inside they were often cold and damp, but there was always a large kitchen. Meals were eaten in the Great Hall.

△ **In medieval towns** there were no proper drains, and people threw their rubbish in the street. Jugglers, actors and others put on entertainments, and there were shops selling all sorts of different goods.

NEW WORDS

⬧ **knight** A man who was brought up to serve as a soldier.

⬧ **lance** A long spear.

⬧ **medieval** To do with the Middle Ages.

⬧ **noble** A person high up the social scale.

⬧ **peasant** A farmer or worker on the land.

⬧ **stained glass** Coloured glass used in windows.

▷ **Stained-glass windows** were used to decorate medieval churches. They often told stories from the Bible, using small pieces of coloured glass held together by lead.

▽ **Knights** took part in tournaments, where they fought against each other on horseback. One knight tried to knock another to the ground by hitting him with his lance.

MAKE A CODE WHEEL

Cut out two card circles, one smaller than the other. Mark them up with the 26 letters and numbers 0 to 9, and pin them together. To write a coded message, choose a key letter, say B. Turn the wheels until A on the outer wheel lines up with B on the inner. Write down the inner letters that line up with the outer letters in your message. To decode, a friend just has to set the wheel to the same key letter.

> ▷ **The ancient Egyptians** used a system of picture writing. Their symbols are called hieroglyphs.

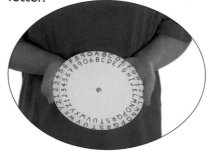

Can flags talk?
Flags can certainly be used to send messages. In the international flag code, there is a different flag for all 26 letters of the English alphabet. Sailors still sometimes use these to talk to others.

> ▷ **Arabic** is the main language of many Arab nations in the Middle East and northern Africa. The Arabic alphabet has 28 symbols and is written from right to left.

△ **Written Japanese** is based on ancient Chinese characters, but the Japanese symbols have developed differently. Japanese children also learn to write gracefully with a brush and ink. This beautiful writing is called calligraphy.

ساحة المهد
MANGER SQUARE

▽ **Russian** has its own alphabet. It has 33 letters and came originally from the Greek alphabet. Russian is related to the Polish and Czech languages.

▽ **Hindi** is the main official language of India, and there are 15 other important Indian languages too. Hindi words are linked with a line running across the top.

АБВГДЕЖЗИ
ЙКЛМНОПР
СТУФХЦЧШ
ЩЪЫЬЭЮЯ

象 王 賊
是 是 奪
玉 玉 取
的 的 王
　 　 的

△ **There are seven** different forms of spoken Chinese. The main form is called Mandarin, or Northern Chinese.

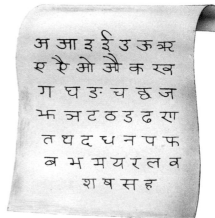
अ आ इ ई उ ऊ ऋ
ए ऐ ओ औ क ख
ग घ ङ च छ ज
झ ञ ट ठ ड ढ
त थ द ध न प फ
ब भ म य र ल व
श ष स ह

Languages of the World

czesc

hello *ni hao* *hola* *namaste*

SIGN LANGUAGE

Native Americans traditionally used sign language, because different tribes had their own spoken language.

A sign language is made up of hand signals.

NEW WORDS

☏ **calligraphy** A beautiful form of handwriting.

☏ **communicate** To pass information to other people, often by talking.

☏ **hieroglyph** A simple picture representing an object or a particular sound.

Language is made up of the words we speak or write down. **Words help us to communicate with each other, to tell each other things.**

There are many different languages, and there are different alphabets for writing them down. People usually learn just one language when they are babies, but they can learn others when they are older.

▽ **This chart** shows the number of people who speak the world's major languages. Millions more people speak Chinese than English.

△ **Here's how different people** say hello. From the left, the languages are English, Chinese, Spanish, Hindi, with Polish above.

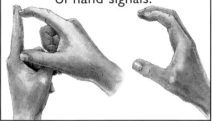

Malay-Indonesian 117m
French 118m
Japanese 124m
German 138m
Portuguese 171m
Bengali 181m
Arabic 192m
Russian 291m
Spanish 331m
Hindi 338m
English 485m
Chinese 845m

-900
-800
-700
-600
-500
-400
-300
-200
-100
-0

◁ **Written Chinese** does not have an alphabet of letters, but is made up of about 50,000 picture symbols. Each symbol, or character, stands for a word or part of a word. These Chinese children already know how to write thousands of characters.

Religions of the World

The world's main religions have existed for thousands of years. During this time, they have tried to explain the world and the meaning of life to their believers.

It is thought that over three quarters of the world's people follow a religion. Religion has been a powerful force in shaping world history, and has inspired many fine buildings, paintings, and music.

▽ **Many Christians** take their babies to church to be baptized, or christened. Babies usually have water sprinkled on them.

△ **Since Roman times,** Jews have gathered to pray at the Wailing Wall in Jerusalem, the capital of Israel. It is actually the Western Wall, which is the last remaining part of the Temple of ancient Jerusalem.

◁ **Buddhism** is based on the teachings of an Indian prince who gave up his riches. The Buddha lived more than 2,500 years ago.

NEW WORDS
baptize To receive a person into the Christian Church with a ceremony.
guru A religious teacher.
turban A head covering worn by Sikhs.

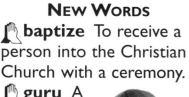

▷ **The River Ganges** is sacred to Hindus. They bathe in the river's waters to wash away their sins.

▽ **The Sikh religion** began in India more than 500 years ago. Sikh men wear a turban to keep their long, uncut hair in place. Sikhs follow the lessons of teachers called gurus.

▷ **Jerusalem** is a holy city for Muslims, the followers of the religion of Islam, as well as for Jews and Christians. The Dome of the Rock is the city's most holy Muslim temple. The place where Muslims pray is called a mosque.

RELIGIOUS SYMBOLS

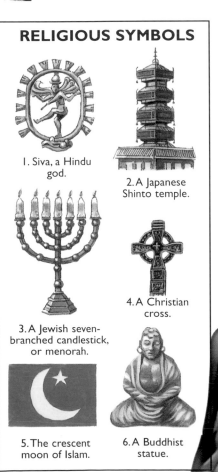

1. Siva, a Hindu god.

2. A Japanese Shinto temple.

3. A Jewish seven-branched candlestick, or menorah.

4. A Christian cross.

5. The crescent moon of Islam.

6. A Buddhist statue.

▽ **Buddhist monks** lead a simple, thoughtful life. They normally own nothing but their robes, a bowl, a razor, and a few personal belongings.

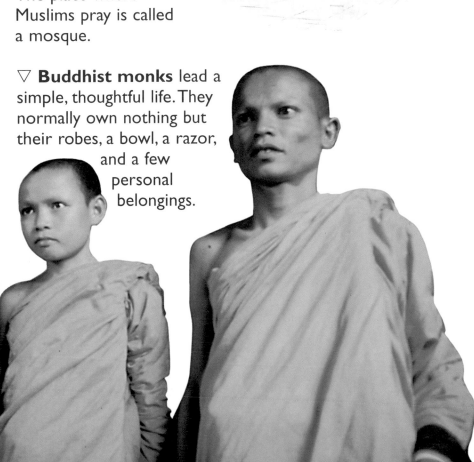

Festivals and Customs

△ **Santa Claus** traditionally brings presents to children at Christmas. He is based on Saint Nicholas, who was a real bishop who lived over 1,600 years ago.

Is there a doll festival?
In Japan there are two doll festivals, one on March 3rd for girls, and another on May 5th for boys. On these days children display the special dolls of their emperors and heroes that were handed down by their parents and grandparents.

Shrove Tuesday is also called Pancake Day. This is because making pancakes was a good way of using up eggs and fat before the start of Lent, when people traditionally fast.

There are many different festivals all around the world. They usually celebrate a person or an event, and many of them happen once a year on special days called holidays.

Festivals are happy occasions, when people dance and dress up. Just like festivals, customs and traditions are handed down from one generation to the next. They are all things that are done the same way, year after year.

▷ **In Mexico,** people remember their dead friends and relatives on the special Day of the Dead.

◁ **On the day of Halloween,** October 31st, children dress up in ghostly costumes, make pumpkin lanterns and play trick-or-treat. It is a day for stories about ghosts, witches and wizards.

▽ **Dragon dancers** weave their way through the streets, celebrating Chinese New Year. This is a time for family parties.

HALLOWEEN FRIEZE
Copy the shapes of a witch, a moon, a bat, an owl and other dark or ghostly things on coloured paper and cut them out. Draw in eyes, stick on decorations and glue the shapes onto a large piece of paper or card. Sprinkle the frieze with glitter for a star-spangled Halloween finish, and put it up in your room.

△ **The world's most famous carnival** is held for four days every year in Rio de Janeiro, Brazil. There are street parades, fancy-dress parties and dances.

✏ **In China**, the end of the New Year season is celebrated by having a special Lantern Festival.

Quiz

1. **What is the name of the** largest gorge in the world? *(page 8)*

2. **Which is the largest** state in the USA? *(page 9)*

3. **What does the name** of the Inuit people mean? *(page 10)*

4. **In which year was the railroad** across America completed? *(page 11)*

5. **Which is the largest country** in South America? *(page 12)*

6. **What is the world's** highest waterfall called? *(page 13)*

7. **What is the main language** of South America? *(page 14)*

8. **Who are** gauchos? *(page 15)*

9. **Which countries** make up Scandinavia? *(page 16)*

10. **Which mountains** separate Europe and Asia? *(page 17)*

11. **In which city** can you see gondoliers? *(page 18)*

12. **What is the name** of a traditional Spanish dance? *(page 19)*

13. **Which is the world's** biggest continent? *(page 20)*

14. **Why was the Great Wall** of China built? *(page 21)*

15. **Which country** has more people than any other? *(page 22)*

16. **What is the traditional form** of Japanese wrestling called? *(page 23)*

17. **Which two seas** are joined by the Suez Canal? *(page 24)*

18. **What is at the top** of Mount Kilimanjaro? *(page 25)*

19. **Where do scientists** believe the earliest humans lived? *(page 26)*

20. **What are** "ships of the desert"? *(page 27)*

21. **What are the three groups** of Pacific Islands called? *(page 28)*

22. **Where is the** Great Barrier Reef? *(page 29)*

23. **Who were** the first Australians? *(page 30)*

24. **What is the international** date line? *(page 31)*

25. **What was inside** the Great Pyramid? *(page 32)*

26. **Which famous ancient Egyptian king** died at the age of 18? *(page 33)*

27. **Who was king** of the ancient Greek gods? *(page 34)*

28. **What did the first** Olympic athletes wear? *(page 35)*

29. **Who was the first** Roman emperor? *(page 36)*

30. **How many soldiers** did a Roman centurion command? *(page 37)*

31. **When were** the Middle Ages? *(page 38)*

32. **What weapons** did knights carry in tournaments? *(page 39)*

33. **How many letters** are there in the Russian alphabet? *(page 40)*

34. **What is the Spanish** for "hello"? *(page 41)*

35. **Where did the Buddha** come from? *(page 42)*

36. **Which river** is sacred to Hindus? *(page 43)*

37. **What is another name** for Pancake Day? *(page 44)*

38. **Where is the world's** most famous carnival held? *(page 45)*

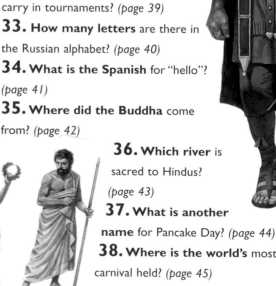

Index

ACKNOWLEDGEMENTS

The publishers wish to thank the following artists who have contributed
to this book:

Janos Marffy Page 9 (C), 13 (CT), 17 (B), 21 (B), 25 (T), 28 (B);
Mike White (Temple Rogers) 10 (BL), 11 (BR), 14 (BR), 15 (CR), 18-19 (CB),
22(TL), 23 (CR), 30 (CL, CR), 34 (T), 35 (CR), 36 (TR), 37 (CR), 39 (BR), 43 (BL),
44 (TR);
Ron Hayward 12 (BL), 16 (CR), 25 (BR), 40 (BL, CB, BR), 41 (CL), 42 (B),
43 (CR), 44 (BR);
Mike Foster (The Maltings Partnership) 11 (CT), 15 (TR), 16 (CL), 21 (TR),
28 (TL), 31 (CR), 35 (TR), 36 (BR), 40 (CL), 41 (T, CR), 44 (CL);
Rob Jakeway 32 (TR);
Richard Hook (Linden Artists) 35 (B);
Michael Welply 38 (B), 39 (T).

The publishers wish to thank the following for supplying photographs
for this book:

AKG Page37 (CL);
E.T. Archive 39 (CR);
Miles Kelly Archives 8 (CL, BL), 9 (CR), 10 (TL), 11 (CL, CR), 12 (BR, CR),
12-13 (CT), 13 (CL), 14 (TR), 15 (BL), 16 (TL, BL), 17 (TL), 18 (CL, TR), 18-19 (C),
19 (TR), 20 (TR, CL, B), 21 (CT), 23 (TR, CL, BR), 24 (CR, BL), 25 (BL),
26 (BL, TR), 27 (CL), 28 (TR), 29 (C, BR), 31 (TR, TL, CL), 32 (BL, CR, BR),
33 (TR, BR), 34 (BL), 36 (CB), 37 (TR, B), 38 (TL), 40 (TR, C, CR), 42 (TR),
43 (TR, BR), 44 (BL), 45 (T, CR);
Panos 27 (TR, CR);
The Stock Market 31 (CB), 41 (BL), 42 (CL), 43 (CL).
All model photography by **Mike Perry at David Lipson Photography Ltd.**

Models in this series:
Lisa Anness, Sophie Clark, Alison Cobb, Edward Delaney, Elizabeth Fallas,
Ryan French, Luke Gilder, Lauren May Headley, Christie Hooper,
Caroline Kelly, Alice McGhee, Daniel Melling, Ryan Oyeyemi, Aaron Phipps,
Eriko Sato, Jack Wallace.

Clothes for model photography supplied by:
Adams Children's Wear